"Perhaps some of the greatest books
were written yawning." — Proust

IT'S TIME

IT'S TIME

POEMS

REGINALD GIBBONS

Louisiana State University Press   Baton Rouge   2002

For Ted Weiss

and remembering
Roland Flint, Tim Dekin, Manuel Ulacia,
Agha Shahid Ali, and Charles Segal

Copyright © 2002 by Reginald Gibbons
All rights reserved
Manufactured in the United States of America
First printing
1 2 3 4 5 Cloth   Paper 5 4 3 2 1
02   03   04   05   06   07   08   09   10   11   11   10   09   08   07   06   05   04   03   02

ISBN 0-8071-2814-7 (cloth); ISBN 0-8071-2815-5 (pbk.)

The author thanks the editors of the following publications, in which were published earlier versions of these poems, sometimes under different titles: *American Poetry Review:* "Birthday," "Down There, If You Look," "Stop"; *Bridge:* "Blue Annunciation," "Finally I Noticed"; *Crazy Horse:* "Poem Including History"; *88:* "Summer"; *A Journal of Contemporary American Poetry:* "Summer"; *Literary Imagination:* "Mortal Men," "Winds"; *Luna:* "Finally I Noticed," "Ghazal"; *Notre Dame Review:* "The Nature of Thought," "Notebook"; *Ontario Review:* "Blue Annunciation," "Winter"; *Pequod:* "Duet"; *Samizdat:* "Avian Migrations"; *Texas Observer:* "Envoi"; *Tikkun:* "A Leap," "Refuge."

"Manifesto Discovered Under a Fringed Gentian" was anthologized in *Power Lines: A Decade of Poetry from Chicago's Guild Complex,* edited by Julie Parson-Nesbitt, Luis Rodriguez, and Michael Warr (Tia Chucha Press, 1999). "Ghazal" was anthologized in *Ravishing DisUnities: Real Ghazals in English,* edited by Agha Shahid Ali (Wesleyan University Press, 2000). "Blue Annunciation," "Ghazal," "I Not I," "Down There, If You Look," and "Envoi" appeared in *Hammer and Grace: A Gathering of Poets,* edited by Heather McHugh and Ellen Bryant Voigt.

The author is grateful to the Alice Berline Kaplan Center for the Humanities of Northwestern University for providing fellowship support during the year in which some of these poems were completed.

The paper in this book meets the guidelines for permanence and durability of the Committee on Production Guidelines for Book Longevity of the Council on Library Resources. ∞

CONTENTS

IT'S TIME

THE STORY

Laid out on the neatly made bed, the blouse you chose
Not to wear. I look
And look at it, to retrieve my soul from the calendar.

Outside, knobby winter
Branches of the buckeye like a profusion of antlers;
Inside, asterisks like stickerburrs clinging here and there to a text.

Later, on the job, I guide small groups up a snowy paradox
Or alone I sound talismanic
Pairs of words in the southwestern part of the morning.

❋

Spiritual bees alight
And feel their way toward us, crowding closer
To see blossoming miracles or accidents in the roads.

Although we never stayed, I wandered with you through
Churches. Like two faint slow
Rays of light drifting through the darkness inside an eye.

❋

I begin a walking tour of the broad fallen kingdom of thought:
There, horses graze and gorse blazes,
Money argues, dogs darken, bogs bark, warps woof.

1

In the noise-shadow of an abandoned acropolis, I visit
A philosophical park. An oak there
Seems the consciousness of the acorn from which it grew.

I decide in favor of shouting in the street, not the secret conference.
I look past the barricades down the avenue. Then I decide
For reason.

Thus I am required to address propositions, such as "Piety
Is wrong." So I must
Crawl like a bug along a line of words bigger than I am.

Tired, I return home to you. You show me
Armfuls of stories and the healing unintended radiations
From the heads of infants.

Down from immensity
The stars come to bang on our roof. Gods and saints
With their hands make gang-signs of the cosmos.

☾

But weightless we orbit
Around a transmitter of images, imaginary numbers, and numberless
Epidemics of illusion, till we hide ourselves away to dream.

A rain of memory falls inside our house but wets nothing.
Fires burn inside singing voices but these singers,
Without fear, see with their mouths, and will watch the night away.

BLUE ANNUNCIATION

Tawny hay bales on
        the tan mown slope

Distant cypresses on hunched
        ridges like black candle flames

The sea as dark as purple grapes

Ozone scent of ordinary
        fierce geraniums and hot
thick pungency of meek petunias

Obsessive announcements of a hidden dove

There's a word for the
        color of the clear sky
but none for the falling-away-
        upward depth of it
that feels too spanning and
        speeding from us
for us ever to have called
        into it in time

And for what purpose down the
        hundred thousand generations—
from carved magic
        bone to machine gun
from daubed red ocher to
        acres of robbed riverbeds—

did our perceiving, when it
        comes into us
fully, into our hollows,
        become in itself such pleasure?

OH

In summer breezes the leaves of the old trees shake.
On the gentle slope the shaded sidewalks are dry.
Under the August afternoon the lake
Answers with both gray and blue the clouds and sky.

I amble along, one hundred years ago
(When with hand tools the house where I live was built),
Till a small poem—shape of both id and ego—
Arrives at the end of a wandering, walking thought.

Immediately the poem feels vertigo, it moves
With a hitch in its gait, it's not convinced it should have been
Given this path, when it would have liked to discover
An unforeseen matriarch or a vague feather or a violin.

At land's edge, tumbled defenses of dumped rocks,
The size of sealed crates and graffiti'd with odd codes
For the strange destinations that they'll never reach,
Till now have kept the lake from the land it erodes

And the land from throwing itself once and for all
Into the lake on an impulse it could no longer suppress.
And the one-hundred-year-old poem, taller on formerly metrical
Tiptoes than the highest rock, scans the horizon for rescue

From this world into which it was born by mistake.
I do not imagine swans flying away for all time
But the town disappearing by winter (while the poem was still trying to make
Sense, poor thing) and scavenger gulls that feed on rhyme.

QUATERNARY

Glaciers that changed
        their minds, receding . . .

The factual historiography of
        the animals and plants
written in layers of
        silt and in tree rings

Scrub forests that entered
        pale meadows, filled them

Meadows that rose into
        full sun out
of forest killed by
        shallow flood

Alien species of
        birds and weeds that
in a mere two
        hundred seasons
resettled this continent

Triumphs without intent
        thus without celebration

And defeats (to which
        the gaze of a
bystander, byflyer,
        byleaper, bystalker—
fixed instead on some
        unaffected prey,
seed, flower—
        remained indifferent)

No necessity of
        choices such as between
Kechua and Spanish

No ideology in
                    the presence now
of dry low
                    weeds that rattle

No pained memory of
                    high leaves that
once made the
                    light tremble

No grief
                    in the last of
a species, clutching
                    a branch, blinking,
alone but not
                    having to understand

SUMMER

Under a front-yard being in full
Infinitely varied leaf—each, no matter
How imperfect, perfectly maple—
I wait, while at an angle to
The upright world rain
Begins to fall and vapor
From the hot wetted street rises
Through and against the rain,

Two motions interpenetrating,
Two metaphors proposing different ideas.

Meanwhile, dipping as the drops of rain
Strike them, this year's leaves say,
"As long as each of us lives, we live—
Whether each form of us is fully
Itself or stunted or eaten by
One creature or by another cut
Or by you sentenced."

Cloud-mist around the earth-bound.
Some idea, at last, where only
An attitude usually is.

"What has been the moment of your being—
You that think? Is your thinking being
The fullness of the form of you?"

Within hearing of a nearby synod
Of some hundreds of stamens convened
For silent sessions day and night
And nodding nay and yea while rain-being
Falls and mist-being rises,
I hesitate to answer.

WINTER

A crow arrives and perches in the tree.
It studies me.
                    It wants to peck my eyes.
Every single neighbor offers me
A gun. I shoot the crow.

Wounded, it falls through branches, dies,
Catching itself, and lands in snow.

But now, still surviving, it walks,
It staggers off, its wings make bright red marks
Like ancient writing, signs of chants and cries.

This is the crow that would have eaten my eyes.
A scavenger, a predator, a thief
Of life.
Yet there it writes, not I, the poem in blood
That no one could not say is good.

TROIS MAZURKAS

1. Anniversary

> à Mme C. M. S.

You are sweet to remember.

Longing finally became belonging,
It turned in
To lingering images and echoes,
The beginning of a story:

Before there was what this is,
Before there was everything,
For sweet instance,
There was still anything—

Which enthralled and frightened.
To choose each other was
To chance more than we could
Comprehend or recall,
So it was to choose to imagine.

How sweet you are to remember.

2. Birth Day

> à Mlle K. E. C.

On your birth night I too, somewhere, was born—
New self who from the old would come to be.

Carried to a new New World by you,
I tried to guide you while you guided me.

To islands of the blossom and the thorn
We voyage, tracing maps that we make new,
Through a blessed bay, over a bad reef,

Saving each other with what we have to give,
As you keep being born—spirit, conscience, belief—
Following a star of dusk and dawn called love.

3. Rubato

à Mlle Martha Argerich

Means: time stolen from one note
and given to another.
So, with strong beats often dis-
placed, since this
dance is not at all a waltz
but surges then holds back, like
feeling, Chopin's mazurkas
for piano make the two hands
sometimes play
a rhythm not exactly
with but somewhat against each
other—the right lagging, drag-
ing a beat or two out but
hastening
to catch up
an instant later, while the
left—so it
is said of Chopin's own left
hand—plays on at a steady
measure of
three, three, three . . .

And you and I—who hear or
don't hear the beat—listen, don't
listen, lose
our sense of time in the forms
of songs that say nothing or
something, someone coughs loudly

to say with
his own unsinging voice that
he refuses song, and we,
what is it we should have done
today that we have to do
tomorrow?

           (All this is wide-
wandering
thought, while she plays—the pianist
stealing time for us from work
and duty, from the tangles
we are caught
in, from the clock ticking and
ticking in our alarmed heads—
the time that
she has no intention of
ever ever giving back.)

FINALLY I NOTICED

All those hats worn neither for warmth nor shade nor safety;

And headdresses—of feathers or snakes,
Of cloth or wood, of shells or horn,
Of skins or even stone—

Olmec, Egyptian, Hindu, Sioux,
Louis Quatorze, Brazilian Carnival—
Hats of men and women, gods and goddesses,
Even those headdresses shaped like the head itself,
Whether that be animal or human;

In rock paintings, the rays, antlers, curved branches,
Ecstatic hair standing straight
Out from the mystic head;

The shining neck-rings raising the
Elegant head to an almost decapitated height
Like a headdress of itself;

Narrow tall masks immensely magnifying the forehead;

Miters, hoods, cowls, turbans, bonnets, wimples, crowns;

High-piled hairstyles;

The plumes or ribands or horsehair tassels on otherwise
Practical helmets of metal, leather, wood, plastic;

The yarmulke, the scarf draped or tied,
Sacred or supposedly secular, put on either to keep
From offending God or to propose
Timidly that God stop
Looking into the human head;

Or, as if conceded by God himself:
The halo
(Now I am getting to it);

And sometimes that which by being opposite is
The same—the monk's tonsure or the head
Shaved clean of all hair and wearing,
Bearing, nothing and so again
The center of attention—

All these shapes of what
We feel
        extends so far
Beyond the head inside which
It happens—

        something sometimes
Enormous but feathery, shaking
In the dance,
        sometimes small but as
Weighty as the world.

NAVY BLUE WOOL POEM
WITH INSIDE POCKET

In wintry spring weather
every country and town
tree stands comfortably
in the whipping cold wind.
But my human being,
still chilled through under my
coverings, brings itself
inside and thinks: about
the bride-price of somewhere
an unavailable
vaccine; about hunger
in the shadow of a
treaty; about a girl
who walked by me wearing
a man's frayed overcoat
and asked me for only
one dollar, just where a
red-feathered songbird was
putting a typical
street corner inside un-
expected musical
quotation marks; about
the friend who turned away
just the other evening
and with a last breath gave
up loving and dying.

NOTEBOOK

(a)

Greedily I write
as wind ruffles the pages something like
wind blowing across the hay stubble
one crow standing alone in the wide field
and I close away my little treasure

That which while
I experience it I
annotate to make it
more fully present to me

Partly to preserve it partly
from loss

Yet wind hay stubble and crows
will outlast they do not need my words

(e)

Repeat:
A human hand
A pencil
Words on paper some salvage of the moment
Then writing is over
and the windy field continues to exist

(i)

Wind across a field

Ruffled black feathers on the back of an unmoving crow indifferent
    to the wind

Wind

(o)

The word "wind"

The wind

In this language I write
the word for it
and also the "the" the wind
doesn't need, the "the" the "the"
doesn't itself point to except
when forced to do so

I force it
and

the written word receding in the
wake of the present moment is
blown backward like a scrap of paper trash
toward the far edge of the field
toward
the
trees there

from field-light day to night-dark woods—
time a gale and the
word like a singing bird unable to return against it

(u)

The sound of the mind in the trees

I NOT I

You cupped the gushing water in my palms
You walked the miles with my determination
You listened for the first sound of night with my ears
You did the job with my sore hands and stumbling feet

You spoke the words with my lips and tongue
You drank with my gulping thirst
You rushed up the wooded slope with my legs and lungs
At the top you felt the cold wind against my skin

You counted your breaths with my attention
Greedily you tasted through my nose
and mouth the scents of flowers and infants
You pushed my breath with my gut into your shout

You canvassed for signatures with my persuasiveness
You hitchhiked to the demonstration with my thumb
With my politics you studied the crowds and speakers
then you walked the real avenues with my questions in mind

You brought forth the images in my thoughts
You beat the blood through my body with my heart
You used my eyes to see the woman's beautiful nakedness
You entered the woman's beautiful *cunnan* with my *dictare*

You lifted the heavy red grief and carried it in my arms
You felt my pain as the stab wounds healed
You groped through my mental fog for the needed word
You lost the thread of my thinking

You took what you wanted with my appetite
You tore and chewed meat and anger with my teeth
You swallowed hard with my throat
You used my bowels to push shit out

To you, things happened in my dreams
You fevered the heat of my desires and fears

With my musicianship you played the piano
You wrote the pages with my right hand

With the excuse of my fatigue you stopped creating
You found it hard to avoid the ambiguity
of statement that permits an easier interpretation
You found it hard to straiten the passage

in order to permit only the difficult interpretation
that is singular, elusive and at least somewhat enduring
You were not a god or a spirit but you arrived through me
You were not I but you arrived only through me

POEM INCLUDING HISTORY

"Europe" began with war or with a poem
chanted in remembrance of warriors:
the thirteenth-century-B.-C.-E. clashing
of swords, gods, kings and verbs.
Like wars of which we know in our own
historical nights and nightmares, were these, too,
fought by men for gain and to sustain illusions?
The Hittite Empire falling,
Mycenaean civilization destroyed,
Egypt attacked by the Sea Peoples.

After another hundred or so full cycles
of the seasons, a raiding invading people
called Dorian "took power" in Greece.
We might imagine of this modern historian's phrase
its lived specificity: its doorway
and cooking fire, its overturned baskets,
spilled oil, lame mule left behind,
shattered amphorae, a blinded child,
quickly bundled small possessions. Many
Hellenes—the most ancient "Greeks"—died or fled.

Europe began with "ethnic cleansing."
The refugees sailed away from the Dorians, east
across the cold sea to where phases of the same moon
shone on different lands, to islands, to where
the same daily journey of the chariot of the sun
cast the same shadows on different ground,
to Asia Minor, leaving Thessaly, Phokis,
Lokris, Boeotia, home places everywhere.
They went to Lesbos and to the Anatolian coast
to enlarge or establish Ionian city-states,

new villages and farmsteads, new temples, to fish
from new harbors of blue water shading
shoreward to turquoise, to make again from clay
the krater, kylix and amphora, to fashion sandals
as before, again at looms to weave, to hammer
soft silver and gold. "Soon afterward"
("soon" in such a chrono-logos of human
lives meaning what?—the elapsed span
of years from seedlings to tall fir trees,
from toddling girl to grandmother,

or maybe twice that or maybe three times?)
the Dorians, following the sea paths
of the refugees whom they themselves had chased out,
sent a new expedition east from Greece
and were watched, they must have believed,
by the unseeable eye of the capricious
immortal sea, the under-ocean god
already named and renamed many times
by those whom he might wreck or save.
Their sea-journey colonized islands of Rhodes and Kos,

the wide mainland plains, high slopes shaded by pines,
and lofty steep stone outcrops along
the Anatolian coast south of the Ionian towns.
Epics that were sung before a dying fire
or intoned by rhapsodes in royal rooms
brought all the peoples into a single
harmonious admiration for heroes, albeit different ones.
Meanwhile, in Anatolia, the Greeks—
Hellenes—encountered, settled
or traded with, intermarried with,

or abducted or murdered
and were abducted or murdered by, etc.,
many peoples who had already been
"displaced," there in Anatolia, by the same
mortal antitheses that had animated
the Dorians to "take power" in Greece,
that birthplace of the idea that all is argument,
debate, contest, conflict—the Mysians,
Phrygians, Carians, Lykians, Leleges,
Pamphylians, Pisidians, Cilicians (Kilikes), many

others.
This effected a mutual Hellenizing
and Asianizing during those many
lifetimes—we could span them in a sentence,
yet each life spanned infinite seasons,
such as between the days of bright buds,
new green, on the tended olive
trees and much later the harvest of ripe
olives: an infinite sameness and varying
of labors, thoughts, meals, prayers.

Between the olive harvest and the pressing of
all the oil only a few days later: another
infinitude, smaller. Between the pressing of
the oil and the pouring of it all into
ruddy amphorae, only a few hours later:
yet another. And even in that one
moment when the amphora mouth
was stopped with cork under the heel
of someone's hand and melted
dripping wax sealed away the green-gold

oil: an infinitude of fluttering inarticulate
thoughts behind the one thought
of the stopping. . . . But eventually all
the Greek-speaking movement into Anatolia
"brought Greeks into conflict with"
other ruling powers. Persian war-journeys
toward Greeks began around 665 B.C.E.
About one hundred years later,
what we now call the "east," mobilized by Kyros
(i.e., Kurush) the Second (i.e., "Cyrus the Great"),

was at war with what we call the "west"
(Greeks—both the Athenians and their enemies,
the Spartans). This strife continued until
481 B.C.E. Oracles were
consulted. Imagining blind Homer's ancient
heroic captains, these hoplites
shrieked war-cries for blood's sake:
thus feats and wounds and fates past bearing and the soul
that breathed its escape out of the death-mouth
even if that was stopped by insulting dirt.

There was so much destruction (especially
of Athens) that it made possible a great period of
culture (about one hundred and fifty years),
of rebuilding and building, of
re-creating and creating new material
splendor and a new splendor of ideas
and practices—in the midst of and despite
or even in some ways dependent on
what a historian of realpolitik of then or now would
merely call "unpleasant," which is to say,

for those who lived it one by one, horrifying,
unendurable, the irreversible and foreverlasting
destruction of young men who bore arms
and of those whom they attacked,
and of houses and stables, and of children
and vineyards, and of scrolls and eyes,
and of temples and mouths.
(Which was also when, at the end
of a hundred years already of writing
down the words of thought and feeling,

war-words and word-wars, Euripides—
to whom the Dorians, the Mycenaeans, the Ionians,
seemed more ancient than he seems to us—
would describe, with apparent admiration
of the far-off past, "fine tall-towered
cities by the salt sea" where "barbarians"—
those who were not Greek,
who spoke other tongues—and Greeks
all lived together. But that idea
made many of his Athenians and makes many

of us Americans, Saudis, French, Russians,
Jews, Palestinians, Serbs, Germans, Boers, Iranians, English,
Chinese, Japanese, Hutu, and so forth and so
forth and so forth shut souls' eyes tight and
loudly praise illusions.) Then where Europe
was born, between and among Greeks
(for even the doubly ancient Dorians had become "Greek"),
the Peloponnesian Wars began—Athens against Sparta.
Keen interlocutors now with keen swords.
But war too is culture.

We could write of its origins, but as with
all history, we can only with difficulty be certain.
Long before Euripides wrote, Homer
chanted. Remembering what he had heard
from older bards, from Ionian great-
grandfathers, from barbarians, and remembering
being hurt, unable to see any more, carried
joggling in his mother's arms as she ran from killers
at dusk and moaned pleas under her breath
till up in a little canyon on the low

sacred mountainside she could hide safely
with his father and older sisters to rest,
only to flee again on the next day, Homer the man
beautifully praised mythical warriors, not his mother.
We could think of how the seedling becomes
a tall straight pine, the toddling girl
grows with it and gives birth, her
daughter grows and gives birth and the newly
pressed gold-green oil is poured
from the unstopped amphora into a small bowl

then ceremonially placed on an altar
in honor of a god or daimonic hero and
the daughter's grown daughter's grown son,
with an illusion and a prayer pushing at his back,
goes away toward some barbaric altar that he
will pollute, some diamond mine that he
will raid, some rifle that he will fire,
some house that he will destroy,
some daughter whom he will rape,
some counterpart whom he will kill.

I praise the gesture of a generous hand
that smooths unequal wrongs into an equal peace,
that would turn the cost of a military aileron
into ivy and guitar strings and terraces of rice.
I praise the kiss, the bowing, the word, that mark
an instant of human time defined by loving.
I celebrate your reluctance to think of harm.
Praise the thought, the reasoning,
the prayer, too, and the tragic play
that portrays the destroyer and does not destroy.

AVIAN MIGRATIONS

1.

Pale gulls stand in the dark plowed fields like delegates.

The scent of the turned earth saturates the air.

Standing among the gulls, two small black overcoats, cawing.

In a long line, close beside each other, cedars seem to have arrived with the intention of awaiting some disclosure.

Beside them on the dusty road the haggard, bearded wanderer is walking, on his way toward some civilization or other, looking down, smoking a cigarette, while in his mind the innumerable words have flocked together and are about to fly south over the smoke of wildfires and cities.

2.

The collection manager of the bird specimens at the natural history museum told of often stopping, on his way to work during spring and fall, at the immense convention building—tall, long and wide—on the shore of Lake Michigan, where on the north side he would gather the bodies of the migratory birds killed by their collisions against the expanse of glass before first light.

The north side, whether in fall or in spring—a puzzle.

Are these particular birds blown off course by winds, and do they return in starlight or dimness before dawn or under dark clouds toward shore, making for the large bulk they might perceive as forest?

They have been flying along this same route for tens of thousands of years, and not yet has their thinking formulated this obstacle of the city that has appeared in the swift stroke of a hundred and fifty cycles of their migration.

3.

Near the state capital, elderly nuns are arriving to be imprisoned.

Outside the penitentiary gates their friends sing songs with them and pray, a man holds up a poster he has made that says "Welcome to Caesar's Palace," and from narrow office windows, high above the ground, the warden's staff are watching.

They wish the laws and judges did not require nuns to arrive like tall waterfowl to be caged for half the year for having chosen to step again into the forbidden precincts of nuclear missiles.

4.

Cries, in every season, left a basement room that lay below the intolerable weight of the whole imprisoning building, and through a heating duct they almost instantly reached a corridor—but already much weakened—and flew to the end of that corridor, where to pass through a door they gave up much of what was left of themselves, and they gained another hallway and a window to the outside, but the window was closed, and after passing through the brittle, merciless glass they attained the open air and they whispered themselves to a leaf of grass and the fallen wing-feather of a sparrow, and finally with the infinitesimal weight of their own exhaustion they sank into the earth, unheard by anyone who would have wanted to try to answer.

5.

There was an interrogator for the chief prefect of the city, a torturer with a nearly infallible sense of the near side of the limits of physical agony, humiliation, and impotent terror, in human beings—a man who was known to his superiors and fellows for his impeccable silence both when at work (others asked the meaningless questions) and afterward, and who under another name wrote poems.

These survived their own era, winging steadily through time like a small flock, but never to return to their own time. Six or sixteen centuries later, when shards of poetry were rediscovered in the unearthed rubble around formerly great buildings, poems by the interrogator were considered to be of especially delicate, memorable beauty, but about their author nothing, not even his false name, was known.

REFUGE

Beyond the suburbs, armed
           bulldozers crush the libraries
Of wildflowers, all religions of
           butterflies are suppressed,
Hamburgers force their way
           even into the forests that
Never before had been
           cut, there they impose new
Administrative districts on
           the bewildered star fields
Of bright trillium that
           constellate the ground. . . .
But farther in, farther for
           a little while yet,
The sister saplings still do
           not tell their myth, they whisper
Warnings to each other, as blue-
           feathered heads abruptly
Look up from their studious reading
           of acorns, tall leafed
Beings breathe out
           benevolence and each grass
Stem no different from
           innumerable others happens
To move in the soft sweet
           air in such a way as
To be fully itself, singular,
           it sways gracefully,
Alone now, alone, unafraid, at
           the center of the universal hour.

THE NATURE OF THOUGHT

The song of the wood thrush
sounds through the summer air
but the air does not hear it.

Against stone

water

moving, but
           the shape of it not moving—

water intricately jumbled, fallen,
splashed, channeled and not
bounded except by the shape of
the shape of itself that it moves through.

MORTAL MEN

for Alan Shapiro

Along a quiet steep rough-cobbled road,
Newly cut weeds and torn green pages
Sweetened the moving air and the light
    Drawn slowly into sunrise
By benevolence, by all that was good, even by gods
    And goddesses.
Early, I hiked uphill to stand in view
Of the seen, silent world and see it.
    Island and ocean.

Then hiking down again, I passed three goats
Tearing silver leaves and a man who had cut
The roadside thistles with a scythe,
    Swinging it, singing, sweaty
    And resting now in shade.
    He greeted me.
    A wary trust, sometimes
Given by a hillside or a person,
Can be accepted, then attempted, too—
    Taken and given in return, by man or woman.

    At the peak,
    Stark-edged against the lifeless soft blue sky,
A walled-in whitewashed island-top belief
Has kept its doors and courtyards, flagstones, roofs enclosed
For ages against town life,
Wild flowers, ruined pagan temples, mule roads, boats,
    And down the slope
On every side, the inky sea of stories:

Symbols of what we still have not thought through.
Whenever I remember that place
I go not to the celibate
        Top of Patmos but
Inside that reach of slow-proceeding pagan time
        Where even nothing
Happens as though it were some thing, and where
The moment is as open as
        The sea between

The islands, where slow- or fast-streaming thought,
For which somehow I am made, makes its way
In currents so a slant-sailed boat
        Can trace the star-marked routes
        Across the sea and through time,
        Through calms and gales,
        And navigate ideas
While the many hands of what is dreamed or real,
Benevolent sometimes, steady this old
        Adventurous far-trading human identity.

        In the light
        Of memory, these floating images
(Rough road, wild ivy, mortal weeds, sea cliffs,
Words with eyes, and torn sweet-scented title pages,
A man in his changing moment)
Become the icons of some green impossible
        Creed requiring
Human capacity to be benign.

In an ancient cave nearby, a hard hallowed man
        Wrote the phantastic revelations
Of the dark beliefs in which I once put trust.
Prophecies and fiats issue still
        From stone-hard flags, stock markets and armed altars. . . .
With both hard hands the plowman shoves the share
        Down through the dry thin dirt
As his mule strains and jerks when the plow catches
On stones and roots. The red-brown undercolor

Of old earth fades in the sun. On my slow walk
Passing behind his field I look back at him a while.
I went to school with hard believers who were always
        Looking back.

⊐⊏⊐

The restless captain of our late Olympic flight,
        Chatting with me in the narrow aisle
As his copilot flew us out of darkness,
Said he'd like to destroy the Parthenon,
        Get rid of all the damn antiquities—
These were the reason Greece was still so backward.
        Greeks live in the past, he said,
Cutting his eyes at me as he sized me up.
He kept the latest *Playboy* in the cockpit.

In spring light, delicate wild poppies bloom
Bright red around the trunks of gray-green olive trees,
Beyond the golden planted barley, and everywhere
        The plow can't reach.

⊐⊏⊐⊏⊐

33

Buildings always know when they
    Are empty: they fade, they seem
Tired, then the inheritors of those
    Who built them unbuild them—
    In some old places,
To pull hard marble down or take it from where it lies
Toppled by earthquakes—not
    To carve again but to chock
It in low new walls or even burn it
    For lime to make whitewash
    Or television fame.

Mythological Kadmos—godlike
Warrior yet still a mortal man,
And himself a fantasy of those
    Who told his story—married
An immortal woman, Harmonía.
    He said that to lie with her
Was a bliss on earth for which there were
No words. And yet however chastely
Men might still wish their goddesses to act,
Doesn't describing their naked beauty already
    Trouble sacred fantasies?
    Something tumbles down.

    On some demolished but still gleaming
    Acropolis of thought,
Language is our Parthenon:
Always in ruins—but unlike stone,
Always rebuilding itself already.
        And not far from it
        In spring light,
        Delicate red
    Poppies bloom at the unnamed foot
Of each gnarled growing gray-green column
And everywhere a poem can't reach.

A LEAP

Not always but
sometimes, sometimes—
I, unmoving,
they, unmoving—
I watch for a
while the sixteen
squared columns of
wood—smooth, polished,
dark, in a dark
room—standing all
together, and
I imagine
others—of type,
of marble, of
red granite, that
like these refuse
to hold any-
thing up—nothing
atop them (no
capitals, no
architraves, no
pediments, no
rafters, no roofs;
no temples, no
courts, no markets,
no banks, spires, or
legislatures,
no slaves, no lost
cause, crops, cannons,
accords, foreign
debts, recessions,
no mandates, no
systems, newscasts,
or calendars):
I begin at
their feet and move

my gaze upward
along them, then
at the tops I
feel the next look
as a leap of
my body off
free columns toward
anything or
anyone freed.

MOTHER

In cobalt and gold light on a hot
Dry day on a metaphysical slope
Pitched toward an Umbrian town
Below, a seven-hundred-year-old
Olive tree exhales from
Her silver-green leaves calm breath

And nearby two brown horses with
Black manes, side by side and facing
Opposite poles of history,
Answer her
With patient blowing from time
To time, as with their long tails they
Flick ever-present flies from
Each other's heads.

The olive tree's splayed wide
Gray trunk half
Curves to make a living
Hollow like
A pelvis, so even though
I am big, I will
Myself to be small, inside it
I curl myself and wait a moment,
I still myself and a phylogeny of feeling

Rushes, evolving through me,
Then I stand up out of the tree onto
The path of dust
And dried horse turds and yet again
I am born. . . .

        Now the hands
Of the horses' thoughts will take
The hands of my thoughts and those
Of the tree's thoughts and together
Will be still on this

Path of our scarred coevolution,
In blue-gold light of a moment
Through which we are
Passing without moving—

The tree slowly, the horses quickly,
I with awareness of how quickly.

STOP

I always like to have a little quiet time after the lunch dishes are

And yesterday when we came in here after we ate we didn't

We both of us wish you could visit more often, but we understand how you

I see in the mirror that I don't look very presentable, it's hard at my age to

Let me brush my hair for just a minute, I'll do it while

Sit there by the window, just push that embroidery

No, to the other side, let me do it, I don't

I sometimes wonder why do I have this mirror in here, I hate

Sometimes it feels like there was someone else who lived my life, and I

I had to quit my business school, nights, those years ago when

In those days I could copy a new dress in the store window as soon

It's as though it all happened to someone else, and I myself haven't gotten

I can remember a job interview, it was at the old City Building, so many
    years ago, there were five

I worked for Mr. Collins till you were born, then he

Well that's the way it was in those days, it wasn't like

But you don't know how strong a mother's love

It puts roots into your own flesh and you can never

Remember the time you hid under my bed and you said

When Gloria and you were only babies—you know, you came six years after
   Billy, he

Of course it would have been easier if things had turned out different for
   your father, because with three of you to

He was a popular man in those days, could have gone into the upstairs
   office—I'm not saying everything was

Oh that was before any of you were born, I don't want

But you've come so far, it's wonderful to have

Although I can never stop wondering what Billy

Who knows?—you can't think about

Late at night sometimes, after your father is asleep, I still

We got a letter from a Colonel somebody, but I

You know I don't like to talk about the

I can't help remembering the going-away party for him, when little Gloria
   gave him those

But please let's not

Stop

Wouldn't you like to go out, see some of your old friends, are you

I have to tell you I never liked that boy because he

No, don't talk about that, I asked you before, when

I want you to tell me what's happened to your old friends—Rod and Morris
  and Phil, and that other boy who

No, not Billy's friends

Your father won't even go visit his grave, but I

Remember when we used to take you with us to that little roadside zoo way
  out in Draco County when you were all

And that family roadhouse near

Shuffleboard, we used to play, on those long narrow strips of cement with

I would drink a beer in those days, but your father

Of course he and I never danced—and when I thought of my mother saving
  so hard for my lessons that she

Madame Isabel, everyone called her, but I

It used to be a nice part of town, before—you know, everything got so

Why don't you go find your father and tell him to pick some tomatoes for

I used to be a great one for gardening but he

You can't understand!—where is Billy

I know I should believe but if he's just nineteen forever then

Where is Gloria for that matter and

Just drifting, for the longest time, and she wouldn't

We were afraid she wasn't

Most of the time you're not even

You will?—will you promise me you'll

I need to take a nap—when I think about some things it makes me

He's probably sitting on the back porch by himself waiting for you, he never

No, I

No, I told you, I

I've told you I don't think it *helps* any to say

Well, I'm a little better than your father, at least, look at him the way he

I got over that, I heard from her again last month, she's

He hasn't talked to her, he won't, since

Why did there have to be

I can't even count all the

I'm all right, I

Would you put that embroidery back where

I'm all right

If I could just

PHILOSOPHY

for S. S. C.

"By affect I understand
            affections of the body,
By which the body's
            power is increased or
Diminished, aided
            or restrained" (Spinoza).
By body sometimes I understand
            the glittering wild flocks
On this shore, singing
            or invading, by which
The city of our love of
            life is increased or
Diminished, brightened
            or made ugly.
By city I understand
            the shattered-glass-spangled
Earth of vacant-lot
            gardens in which our
Love of light is
            broken on human harm or
Sustained on flashing hope.
            By light I understand
This dented fixture on
            a small porch,
Because of which, when it
            shines, the night can
Come no nearer, although
            when it is burnt out
It pours more darkness
            into darkness.
By contradiction I understand
            my history with you
Who came to me then
            taught me to invite you,
Who flew into my
            night space to bring me

43

What I had not taken,
                who gave me a generation when
I had not thought to give myself
                to one, who grew into
Imagined feeling till
                it was as granted as a
Bird or a bottle or a lamp.
                By love I understand
A longing in the spirit
                because of which we offer ourselves
For the thriving of the other,
                word for word, glittering
Inner world for world.

MANIFESTO DISCOVERED UNDER
A FRINGED GENTIAN

On the foundational dark silence
      of the forest
And without need
      of worshipers
Temples grow with supple sculptures
      of reaching branches,
With columns
      of air and live sap decorated with living
Friezes, moving scenes in the lives
      of leaves.

Therefore proclaim with the voice
      of moss
An inviolable protectorate
      of wrens
And another, other-continental,
      of toucans.

Confer most-favored status, for the trade in air,
On all remaining mountainsides.
                          Array in fractal
Regiments the sands and grasses
To guard the weary shorelines.
                 Anoint
With last twilights those rivers which, if they are still
Believers, may be reborn.
               Dispatch
Bottom-vigilant finned inspectors to patrol
The poisoned deltas and lake bottoms
And sea depths.
          Sort
Through the gull-shadowed garbage that has buried
Jaguar nations
      of the badger, frog and trout,
And tie the old tin cans
      of rusting gold mines

To the long tails
       of CEOs.
              Lock down the wilding
International Dietary Fund and transsovereign corporations
On regimens
       of clean water and animal crackers.

Herewith we abolish the practice
       of board-feet and clear-cuts,
Hereby we establish the free speech
       of bristlecone branches and Lepidoptera,
Hereafter we will publish only anthologies
       of wildflowers,
We here and now enjoin all poisoning
       of wolves, winged fish-eaters, orchids and heads.

DUET

1.

You will see sometimes in photos
Of human beings who have looked
Into the camera in order to substitute
Their flat likeness, on some future day,
For their presence, the chin resting on the heel of
The hand, the flat of fingers against
The cheek, or thumb and fingers
Propping the head as if to display it
Or offer it to another.

You will notice, also,
When you are with others, the hand
That touches the forehead, the chin, the hair;
The finger across the lips—

                           The body
Keeps returning mind
                   to the head
From the hands,
                 where mind keeps
Heading because it too feels

Desire and it too hungers
For effects of touch and also because
It is
      tired of itself and
Of thinking about what needs to be done,
About tomorrow the cleaners and the grocery,

Tired of remembering
Yesterday the casualties and sentences
Of description and death, tired of having

Forgotten the good umbrella on the bus
And names; there are
Many thoughts to be thought about money,

About faces, about lies;
And also about everything the mind has
To keep keeping away
From itself by keeping it entirely to
Itself, every thing the mind must
Behold with closed mind's eyes, all
The keen anniversaries of the unconscious.

2.

Meanwhile the hand is trying to think.
If only it could utter with its own tongue.
If only it were not at best
A gifted puppet, a flexing
Mute with expressive gestures.

If only it could tell of its wrinkled longing
To plan some great work and send
Others to practice or accomplish it.

POTTER IN RETROSPECT

Fire-glow of a kiln sighing
in northern winter
when work goes on past
the early hour of
the sunset outside.
                    Near the
kiln, alone and ill-
lit, Wally at his
wheel, making more pots
and plates to be glazed then fired
and in far-off summer sold
to tourists.
                    The lightless still
corners over there and there,
piled with stuff.
                    A converted
board-and-batten barn
beside a road and mowed fields,
his dusty studio, a
quarter-mile from the next place.

Beyond the surrounding fields,
woods.
                    Overhead everywhere
the grains-of-salt stars
and unintelligible
infinities that make us
feel infinitesimal,
and the broad still splash
of star-hot milk spilled before
human time began.
                    Reaching
from the north halfway
to the zenith, the pale green
diaphanous curtains of
the aurora slowly and
expressively fluttering
in a solar wind.

Up the road, underground,
                              where
there's no light, Donna's substance
has begun
to interpenetrate the
numberless grains of
everything else that there is.

Inside, where cold shadow and
dim light keep Wally, wearing
an old flannel shirt and jeans,
company, he pushes his
spinning clay toward a fine
or at least a clean,
serviceable shape
that he likes, and likes making,
and at his touch it rises
and moves but not quite like life.

She would have painted the glaze.
He has a lot of unglazed
pieces on his sagging shelves.

It is very quiet. There's
only that all-but-
inaudible hot
kiln and the turning
wheel. Wally's appointment—of
which none of us, not even
he, has any inkling yet—
with Donna's ground is
not six months away. The pale
fire-bricks have cooled from white and
yellow to orange, and to
anyone who saw them now
they would seem cheerful.

NOT FOR NOTHING

Nothing is more peaceful
            than the water horizon
Even nothing is not more
            peaceful than the water horizon
that I feel inside my self reaching
            from shoulder to shoulder in
            me where small as I am I am widest

Nothing is more harmonious than
            the slow C-sharp-major piano arpeggio
Even nothing is not more harmonious
            than the slow C-sharp-major arpeggio
that I hear inside my self sounding from
            shoulder to shoulder in
            me where dissonant as I am I
            arrive at my cadence

Nothing is more good-hearted than the
            northern laughter of the glittering
            tall bright poplars standing close
            together at the green
            edge of a sunny meadow
Nothing cannot have a heart of laughter like the
            glittering stand of tall narrow
            poplars at the far edge of
            a green meadow in breezy summer sun
that I am warmed by from shoulder to
            shoulder within my
            self where heavy and sorrowful as
            I am I become light

Nothing is more loving than what your eyes give me
            in a long instant of your
            gaze apart from all world
For nothing could never be loving

And even an instant of your
                deep gaze, which sometimes seems to
                come from the past, like a star's,
                gives to my own being from shoulder
                to shoulder what full fills me where
                angry or dissonant or sad or alone
                as I have been, I may yet not be

GHAZAL

Archaeologist of feeling, would-be soothsayer of candor,
I work in the sun while I listen for thunder.

I see a coyote trot across a meadow slope, alert and calm,
Like a mind for both the wild rose and the soaring condor.

Time that crawls over everything turns what is
To what was, and creates in us our sense of wonder.

We make love and unmake it, and we ask,
Why did she spurn him? Why did he wound her?

In summer, worshiped sunlight comes clear through green stems
To praise the exploring ant whose only work is to wander.

In autumn, willow leaves migrate to the ground, the geese
Fall southward, a letter homes to me marked "Return to Sender."

Some poplar that lives about as long as I will stand for me,
Will wait in line as I write in lines, until we both go under.

If there comes a day when I can advance no further,
It's because on that day I have no father, no mother, no founder.

I slant through wildernesses and cities of our common cause
That say, Reg, you must be persistent, undiscouraged, and tender.

BLACK-&-WHITE

(Bialystok or Lodz or somewhere)

1. Positive

As though I could look at the
photos that I have not, that
no one has, inherited.
But imagination, like

memory, can provide an
origin. A photograph
that does not exist, a man
who existed: *Sir, don't we*

have to bring the image of
you through forgetting, through burnt
borders, along red roads from
that moment I am trying

to imagine you out of?
I am sorry you received
few letters from your sons, who
emigrated. I know that

someone said you wept on one
green evening when a boy came
running with a letter from
a faraway daughter-in-

law in the country in which
I would much later be born.
When I hold this photo that
no one took, I ask: Which one

event in all the never-
to-be-written histories
makes you squint your eyes in self-
defense? The blue leaden late-

afternoon light pushes at
everything around you, is
inescapable. Maybe
you have hidden bread under

your black coat and somewhere you
are awaited. Even I
can see that your fear is not
only for yourself. Behind

him the wide empty cobble-
stone street narrows between tall
flint offices and granite
apartment houses about

to turn their backs. Abruptly
breaking the quiet—nearby
but out of sight in some rich
kitchen—a white goose gets one

wing free and beats at the knife.
The muffled noise of it, the
exasperated patience
in its executioner's

swearing, audible in the
street, ends. The old man has put
one hand in his long beard—white
against his grave overcoat.

2. Negative

In the negative of this
photo, the beard would have been
black, as when he was young. It
would have lain softly against

the incomprehensible
white of an impossible
coat. That negative must have
been of happiness, since this

developed photo is of
fright. And around him there must
have been a family at
least somewhat loving and friends

who did not yet know that their
fate would be to survive. And
in some doubly unreal day
dream he scarcely could permit

himself amidst the unreal
reality he had no
choice of, the peach and ocher
of bright Italian noontime

warmed him, children were at play
in an outdoor restaurant as
he and his wife, his brothers
and their wives, accepted slow

generous ceremonies
of a meal, not believing
there was holier wine than
the unblessed vintage that the

young untroubled waiter brought
them. Worship or none is not
the issue anymore. On
his gray street corner, though, he

is leaning away in this
forbidden zone, alone. My
make-believe camera has just
biopsied his fear of some

[right adjective not found] *it*
needing only the slightest
start to begin growing, once
more. Abruptly he turns and

as fast as an old man can
walk, he walks away down one
of those narrowing streets that
seems no place to hide. He hides.

I don't call out *Please come back!*
since I can do nothing in
unreal time. A photo that
does not exist began my

reminiscence of one man
whom no one now remembers,
it has kept me at this green
creating of what fails to

be true, although there is still
that which can be true. Now it
is colder. Gray wind of it
is piercing all mourning thought.

DOWN THERE, IF YOU LOOK

Standing lightly, precariously, almost
Floating, don't
Shift your weight even slightly,
Over jagged raw holes in the floor
Of time.
        Down there, if you look . . .

Down there, blue clouds float against
A white sky; great walls and high buildings
Are only deep muddy ditches at the bottom of which
Squatting women are taking their babies
Back into their wombs and standing men
Tilt their heads up as they eat
Long floating ribbons of words.

WINDS

1.

My breath flutters a scrap of onion paper on which are printed words preserved from an ancient time. A leaf outside my closed window, inscribed with the signatures of rain and dust, is also fluttering, it turns, it announces a storm.

2.

How small the world was when it felt large.

When Utnapishtim was given immortality by the gods because he had survived the flood.

When he "knew how things were, in the beginning," before the world had become crowded.

When what happened in the village of Mykenai happened to the world.

When Siddhartha Gautama got up from his meditation at the foot of the sacred tree.

When wrong winds blew up gray-white waves and intrepid Jesus walked across them to the New World.

When in a Tewa Pueblo Blue Corn Woman watched over the naming of each child.

3.

At the scenic overlook with historical marker, as dark storm-clouds approached, several middle-aged women got out of a car and walked arm in arm against the warm high wind rising toward them at the edge of a steep promontory over the valley and they shrieked their laughter of pleasure and mild shock and defiance as the gusts pushed their full summer skirts around and through their legs.

4.

Some surplus of meaning like small spontaneous flame will sometimes kindle from words put next to each other, whipped by gusts of attention and of the unforeseen. Of the possible, the unacknowledged, the repressed, the lost, the liberated, the desired, the unrealized, the commanded, the performed, the uncanny, the obvious, the feared, the playful, the unlawful, the forbidden, the unknown, the withheld, the worshiped, the reviled, the uncontrollable, the thwarted, the despised, the genetic, the generic *(go slowly, now),* the consumed, the secret, the conquered, the unwitting, the perverse, the required, the expected, the fleeting, the mourned, the unbidden, the inarticulate, the impossible, the real, the discovered, the given, the masked, the unpremeditated, the withdrawn, the tentative, the contemned, the inherited *(go slowly!),* the escaped, the inexhaustible, the rejected, the long-meditated, the hoped-for, the sought-for, the fled-from, the beloved.

5.

From inside, a woman opened the door, she came out, she gestured to me to enter, then she followed me in and pulled the door shut behind her. The dimness was a kind of visual echo of the silence. To one side were windows, with shades pulled down and curtains hanging in front of them. The daylight leaking in around the edges of the curtains was enough to show that there was nothing at all in this space, neither on the wooden floor nor on the white walls. The woman reached behind the curtains and opened the windows; then a wind outside began to make the curtains billow toward us. I saw that on the wall opposite the door through which I had entered, there was another curtain, the size of a door, and perhaps a door stood behind it. She went to the curtain and made as if to pull it aside, gesturing for me to come and enter. I spoke for the first time, saying, But what is *this* room for? My voice resounding in the bare emptiness. The curtains swelling and slipping. This room, she said, is to make manifest your transition to the next.

ENVOI

Go, little book, tell of

Rainstorm thunderclap; icy gale; breaking waves;

The rushing movement out there—

Markets; threshers; presses; lobbies and hallways—

Against which we feel the stillness inside us;

Snow quiet; clear night sky; northern summer dawn;

The stillness out there—

Empty barns and shipyards; construction sites and kitchens at three A.M.—

Against which we feel the rushing inside us.

NOTES

"**The Story**": The last line borrows a phrase and a feeling from Emily Dickinson, #471. (Hi, Mom!!)

"**Navy Blue Wool Poem with Inside Pocket**": in memory of Tim Dekin.

"**I Not I**": *cunnan*—Old English word for "to know"; *dictare*—Latin word for "to say often, to assert."

"**Mortal Men**": An ancient Greek ode such as those sung by the chorus in a dramatic tragedy is usually made up of paired stanzas, called strophe and antistrophe, in which the latter exactly matches the former, line by line, in meter while at the same time presenting a contrast of some sort to it, such as of mood or subject. Sometimes an ode consists of more than one such pair of stanzas; it may also end with an epode—a final stanza that does not resemble the others formally, and which turns the poem once more.

"**A Leap**" describes a kind of installation—the plain wood columns among which one passes after entering through a door the small gallery (#109) designed by Tadao Ando, in the Art Institute of Chicago. Yes, of course—but the superb Art Institute too is supported metaphorically by columns.

"**Ghazal**": in memory of Agha Shahid Ali.

"**Potter in Retrospect**": in memory of Wallace Wold.

"Winds": Utnapishtim is a hero of the prehistoric Sumerian Gilgamesh epic. Mykenai is Mycenae in the familiar but distorting Latinized spelling—the small Greek polis ruled by Agamemnon; after killing his daughter as a sacrifice to gods, he departed across the sea to wage war on Ionian Troy; he returned to Mykenai only to be murdered by his wife Klytemnestra. The mythical stories in Homer's epics derive from Agamemnon's decision to wage war with and for his brother Menelaos, over Menelaos' stolen wife, Helen, and Western literature in turn derives from Homer. Siddhartha Gautama: the proper name of Buddha, before his enlightenment. The Tewa are a Pueblo people in the American Southwest.